Strategic Planning

Process, Templates and

Effective Implementation

by Edward Robertson

Published by: Edward Robertson

ISBN: 978-0-9952925-4-3

Any web addresses or links contained in this book may have changed or been discontinued since its publication.

Cover design by Jolanta Robertson
Updated June 2024

Table of Contents

Preface

Why do so many strategic plans end up on the shelf?

It's curious, given that strategic planning is among the most popular of management tools. Evidently, plans that work are sorely needed: entrepreneurs must convince potential investors; small businesses must chart a path, even to survive; and government agencies and non-profits are accountable. Everyone must show how they will face an uncertain future.

The underlying trouble is often that planning is rather unstructured, and yields nothing but a re-hash of familiar ideas, or a confusion of disparate issues. Even if the content is innovative, documented plans alone cannot overcome a mysterious and maddening "implementation gap."

Many firms opt for no plans at all, essentially because their decision-making is based on the force of personalities, not systems or methods. Further, the need for agility and fast scale-up would seem to make formal strategic planning obsolete. But lack of planning ranks high among the reasons for the failure rate of new firms and management initiatives in all domains. The price of altogether ignoring rational planning is very high.

I have seen all this first hand as a researcher, consultant, and manager. My story involves helping to lead a manufacturing operation from a "mom-and-pop" state of affairs to Business of the Year. I also had success as senior manager of a government-wide risk management program.

I will share the stories, but what I want to emphasize along the way are principles. I want readers to consider the generic principles involved and adapt them, rather than look for a rigid formula to be slavishly copied. I think that success in organizational work is determined by the interplay between universal precepts and individual judgment.

The first principle is that strategic planning is *conceptually different* from other types of planning and from various management techniques. For this reason I first establish the rationale for strategic planning; its definition; its relation to other types of planning; and its distinct value as an exercise.

The Introduction is rather long, as I want to explain the role of other types of planning and management disciplines, as well as the common reasons for business failure. The reader/practitioner will then have a solid understanding of "The Why" of strategic planning in order to confidently lead the initiative.

Thank you to my editor Martin Gavin; my critical readers, including my former inspirational collaborator in organizational change Trevor Harmon, and my talented partner Jolanta Robertson for the cover design. I invite readers to send queries and comments to ertech@shaw.ca.

Edward Robertson
Victoria, Canada
June 2024

List of Diagrams and Templates

Introduction – Rationale for Strategic Planning

Three types of plans.
Startups and early stage firms: reasons for failure.
Small businesses and chronic dysfunction.
Internal organizational planning: building scalable systems.
Management disciplines leading to profound change.
Strategic planning and business agility.
Management tools and techniques.
Recap.
Strategic planning and firm performance.
Strategic planning: definition.
The Why: the case for strategic planning.
Plan of this book.

Three types of plans.

The organization's plans are of three essential types:

- The *strategic plan* (our main subject) builds a background of business intelligence, defines the identity of the firm, and develops its overarching goals.

- The *internal organizational plan* is the design of functions and departments, perhaps utilizing one or another management discipline, technique, or method.

- The *operational plan* is the set of intended activities of business units/departments to pursue the strategic goals.

I hope this typology clarifies things for you immediately. Perhaps you have spent time in planning meetings where the discussion goes round in circles. People tend to mix up plans of different levels and types, leading to confusion and giving planning a bad name.

The principle in this schema is that *you must distinguish the organizational level, content, scope and time frame of the plan in question*. Now, the three types of plans (fig. 1) do interact and can be concurrent. But conceptually, the strategic plan comes first. The other two flow from it.

Figure 1. Three types of organizational planning.

Startups and early stage firms: reasons for failure.
Does planning forestall business failure? Yes, it can definitely help.

In a review of 22 prior studies of business collapse, supplemented by interviews with 100 failed entrepreneurs, one author (Lussier 1996) identified several points of failure. A more recent study (CB Insights 2018) similarly gave 100 post-mortem reports. Drawing on both sources (see them for statistics), I list here major reasons for business failure:

- Undercapitalization at the outset

- Inadequate record keeping and financial controls; cash shortfall

- Deficient management team: lack of prior industry experience or management experience

- Lack of specific business plans

- Failure to use professional advisors

- Failure to ascertain market need for product; product itself is deficient

- Out-competed; pricing/costing issues

- Failure to establish a scalable business model

Caution must be used in judging one's own situation. What the studies actually show is that no single factor absolutely determines business success. But certain important points of agreement are evident among the study results.

So we hasten to ask: How should entrepreneurs regard strategic planning itself?

In the review article mentioned, *lack of specific business plans* ranked among the top five (of 14) reasons for business failure—*virtually equivalent in importance to adequate capitalization and management experience.* Yet, not one of 200 failed entrepreneurs interviewed identified the issue!

We might safely conclude that many of the respondents ignored a business plan, but did not see the consequences. Many of the reasons for failure are closely affected by planning, or lack thereof. Potential investors, for their part, favour well-rounded business leaders who show a planned approach. This means that entrepreneurs must present evidence of:

- market needs;
- functioning prototypes;
- profitable business model;
- researched trends and conditions;
- reasoned revenue projections.

Moreover, entrepreneurs must personally have depth and resilience. They need grounding in guiding values and a distinct aim. If all this is demonstrated in a strategic plan, then angel investors and venture capitalists are more likely to think, "Here's a startup I can work with!"

For example, Catalyst is a Canadian early stage pharmaceutical technology firm. The CEO (a pharmacist) explained in a presentation I attended a chronic problem in drug delivery, and showed his long personal commitment to solving it. He demonstrated his command of stakeholder relations and understanding of the nuances of the market. These enduring and strategic elements went beyond the immediate technology solution and gave depth and credibility to his plan.

Small businesses and chronic dysfunction.

Many informally run businesses (or "mom-and-pop shops") are relatively established, and yet share a common fate: at a certain point in their trajectory, things start to go badly.

Sales decline due to shifts in the market and undetected competition. Alternatively, the firm becomes the victim of its own success: growing demand starts to strain its operations. The firm runs more and more at full capacity, like a race car hurtling around the track at top speed. New production or demands for innovation cannot be met; lead times increase. Product quality deteriorates, and existing customers cannot get timely service. Since there is little spare capacity, mistakes become more frequent.

Potential customers turn away, and key people start to leave the firm. Morale and profits decline. Reactive management is the norm. Operations run without formal controls or standards until their inefficiencies become critical. Management has a one-dimensional response: to cut costs.

The diagrams in Figure 2 show the possible trajectories of the business, and the effects of over-strained operations.

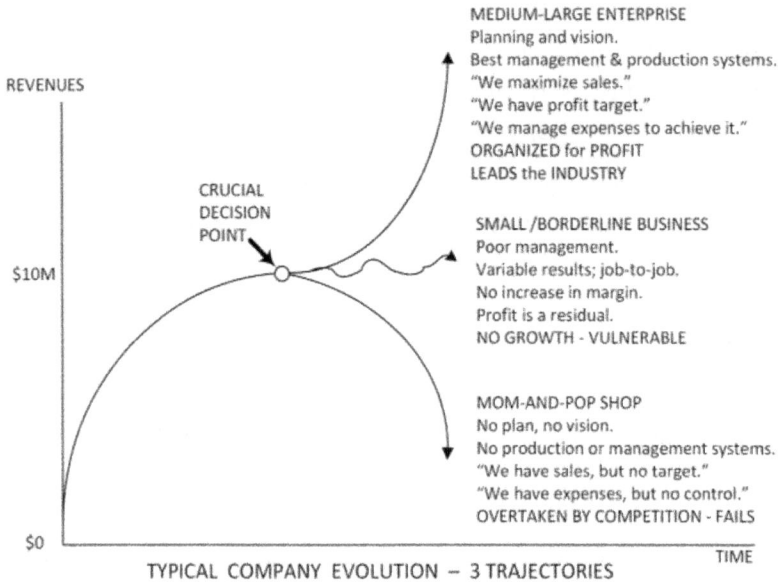

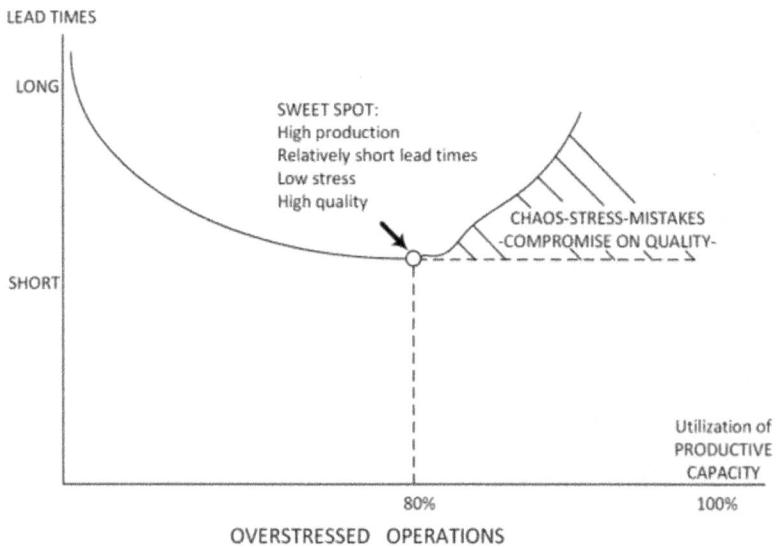

REVENUES

MEDIUM-LARGE ENTERPRISE
Planning and vision.
Best management & production systems.
"We maximize sales."
"We have profit target."
"We manage expenses to achieve it."
ORGANIZED for PROFIT
LEADS the INDUSTRY

CRUCIAL
DECISION
POINT

SMALL /BORDERLINE BUSINESS
Poor management.
Variable results; job-to-job.
No increase in margin.
Profit is a residual.
NO GROWTH - VULNERABLE

$10M

MOM-AND-POP SHOP
No plan, no vision.
No production or management systems.
"We have sales, but no target."
"We have expenses, but no control."
OVERTAKEN BY COMPETITION - FAILS

$0

TIME

TYPICAL COMPANY EVOLUTION – 3 TRAJECTORIES

LEAD TIMES

LONG

SWEET SPOT:
High production
Relatively short lead times
Low stress
High quality

CHAOS-STRESS-MISTAKES
-COMPROMISE ON QUALITY-

SHORT

Utilization of
PRODUCTIVE
CAPACITY

80%   100%

OVERSTRESSED OPERATIONS

Figure 2. Small business evolution and overstressed operations.

A small business needs to envision the proper development of internal systems, which we will now review.

Internal organizational planning: building scalable systems. Let us differentiate strategic planning from the *internal organizational plan*, which has these elements:

a) Management team
b) Corporate structure
c) Financial strategy
d) Business model
e) Operations
f) Facilities
g) Product/program design
h) Information infrastructure
i) HR policies

Although not our core topic, let's consider each element of the internal planning:

a) Management team. It is said that the strength of the management team is the most important factor determining success, because an extraordinary team can work together through adversity. The entrepreneurial skill set includes both product knowledge and business expertise. The best teams will research, create and pursue plans.

b) Corporate structure. This includes the legal constitution (e.g., limited partnership or corporation); the Board of Directors; shareholders agreement; bylaws; charter; etc.

Select board members and advisors with skill sets oriented to the business and complementary backgrounds; be sure to define clearly their roles, responsibilities and deliverables.

> Despite the depth of knowledge and expertise that an advisory board can offer, surprisingly few Canadians use them.
> ~Jenna Sedmak, smestrategy.net

Ownership structure, control, voting rights, compensation, and so on, must be defined. One key point is to recognize the complexity of mechanisms available to coordinate and balance the interests of management, founders and early investors. Neglect of this can significantly disenfranchise one or another party as the firm matures. It demands nothing less than "extensive scenario analysis detailing the possible effects of adverse events" (Stathis 2004).

c) Financial strategy. A projection of capital needs sets out a plan of successive capital raises employing equity and/or debt and derivatives. A cash management plan is crucial to ensure liquidity. Beyond payroll and AP/AR (accounts payable/accounts receivable), financial management must produce ratios to help track the business performance.

d) Business model. This is the method of engagement with the market: how will the business make money?

Investigate the innovative arrangements for business models that are possible in your industry. Let's digress just long enough to cover two examples: CRM (customer relationship management) and online platforms.

A business that is *customer-centred* can build a list of subscribers and serve their needs, e.g., product or process consultation, technical training, software as a service, and access to ancillary products at a discount. Converting one-time clients to loyal followers by meeting their evolving demands reduces turnover and generates recurring revenue. This is a business model distinctly different from focusing just on the marketing of a single uniform product.

Online platforms allow firms to outsource services like advertising, manufacturing, distribution, order fulfillment, and so on. There are considerable advantages (and some risks) associated with using, for example, Amazon's global marketplace. But if you decide to solve all distribution problems by going through Amazon, keep in mind that it doesn't guarantee results. Rather, "one's brand strength, integrity and value"—notice these are defined in the strategic planning process!—are still the first requirements for success (Lewis, 2016).

e) Operations. These obviously vary widely by business type, while common support functions include accounting, administration and HR. These can be outsourced. I have seen even core functions (e.g., a design team) outsourced through an employment agency. In this case not only did the firm save payroll taxes and overhead, but the designers themselves took home more pay than they would have been able to negotiate for themselves as salaried employees.

Generally, operations need to be optimized for efficiency, while maintaining high quality of products and services. This involves management practices and disciplines (described in the next section). The point is: the early stage organization needs to set up systems for all functions that are capable of developing into a *mature practice. Aim for proven methodologies, industry-standard systems and formats, extant knowledge and training.* This makes the business scalable.

The principle applies to administrative and technical matters, and to operations relying on "people skills", relationship building, sales and negotiation. For example, my former director had us take facilitation training as part of the onboarding process (good idea!). This ensured a consistent and professional approach by all staff to facilitated sessions with clients.

f) **Facilities.** Infrastructure essential to the operation, notably in IT, is the source of frequent delays and down time. Set up reviews, checklists and *preventive maintenance* of buildings, facilities, systems, software and equipment. Progressive office space planning permitting work at home is becoming the norm in order to attract talent and retain employees.

g) Program and product design. Pay attention to R&D and a structured innovation program as a planned competency, not just as a matter of the initial market entry. Searches for market niches, pain points and new industry developments must be a core discipline, complemented by ideation exercises, proof of concept and greenhousing. Develop partnerships and other channels for market testing.

h) IT architecture. Data management and information technology, including communications devices, require a comprehensive architecture to define standards, coordinate growth, manage risk, and control total cost of ownership.

i) HR policies. Human resources must support a progressive culture, including retention through a wellness and rewards program, professional development and specialized training.

To summarize: when designing internal business functions of the small enterprise, try to anticipate the mature practice—precisely in order to avoid the failed trajectory of dysfunctional companies outlined above.

Without a doubt the most troublesome, time-consuming, and (what should have been) needless work I have done in several companies is to deal with random and disorganized legacy processes and scattered information, often stored in incompatible formats. Of course, technological change will make some of this re-work inevitable. However, very often early efforts were not made to set up authoritative and robust records management rules; I mean file naming and information storage conventions, backup procedures and numbering systems for clients, jobs, products, parts or drawings, as well as set procedures for common routines.

In technical and administrative processes, do not let workflow remain haphazard. This opens the door to inefficiencies in the form of lost information and missteps. Instead, define the routing and documentation for claims, quotes, sales orders, work orders, drawing release, change orders, shut-downs, security checks and similar repeated tasks. Each aspect is then trackable and accountable.

This is not to say that methods are set and never evolve. On the contrary, the point is to have systems *that can evolve*, beginning as "low-tech" processes that are defined, well understood by staff, repeatable, and tested. This gives you a basis to select the most appropriate technologies. Be sure to use industry standard file formats and data models that can be relatively easily migrated to new and upgraded systems.

In sum: we want to build *scalable systems* and thereby position the firm for growth, rather than unwittingly build in limitations that will be incredibly difficult and expensive to fix retrospectively. Ignoring this can make such a mess that the firm is rendered neither scalable nor even investable.

Now, a project to profoundly change the character of internal functions can constitute a *strategic goal* (see next).

Management disciplines leading to profound change.
The research effort within strategic planning can identify management disciplines that, if properly implemented, profoundly change internal business processes. They should be assessed to determine their appropriateness and feasibility as strategic goals. Examples follow:

Enterprise risk management. ERM answers the demand for accountability and program efficacy by managing all risk associated with goals and objectives. It goes beyond the conventional categories of insurance and financial controls.

Enterprise resource planning. An ERP system is needed in a manufacturing operation to rationalize inventory, material flow and costs. Implementation is expensive, and commonly fails or underdelivers when change management is ignored.

Crucial Conversations.™ A firm called VitalSmarts has developed an extended program to help people engage effectively with others and to manifest accountability.

Knowledge management. This discipline, pioneered by McKinsey & Company, captures and distributes significant information learned on the job so that it becomes common knowledge among staff. It is related to organizational learning (see Senge 2006).

Lean manufacturing (including Total Quality and Quality at the Source) offers a methodology to improve productivity and the working culture through better organization, workflow efficiency, standards and behavioural change.

Lean startup. Originally a software development methodology, it relies on quick and iterative product development cycles. Note that experimentation with one's customers may not be feasible in all fields.

Quick Response Manufacturing.™ This methodology, complete with supporting research and training, rationalizes processes to drastically cut lead times (Suri 1998).

Agile is a software development method (applicable to other processes) including the "Scrum framework," signifying "ability to quickly adapt to or even anticipate and lead change" (Kelly 2015).

Are business agility and strategic planning itself at odds? As this is a common question; we address it next.

Strategic planning and business agility.

Business agility is "the ability of an organization to rapidly adapt to market and environmental changes in productive and cost-effective ways" (Wikipedia). Strategic planning is sometimes shunned as a long, drawn-out process, which will be overtaken by rapidly shifting market demands. The cry is "Strategic planning is dead!" Rapid growth and fast product development are prized, especially in high-tech.

Agility, however, does not signify either reacting impulsively to every signal in the environment, or changing one's core values at every turn. Rather, it is a crafted strategy to deal with variability quickly—but also intelligently.

At a manufacturing firm, where I led organizational change, we faced the problem of constant requests for innovative products. This disrupted normal production and led to very uneven results: requests were accepted without criteria; response times were wildly erratic; costing (and resultant profit) were a residual surprise; scheduling was upset, and the competing demands for resources caused constant friction. No wonder people would come up to me on the shop floor and say: "Ed, get me out of the chaos!"

We finally created a process which, in effect, asked: a. Does the candidate project align with our desired product mix?; b. Can it be directed into our standard production stream (even with some customization)?; and, if accepted instead as an innovation challenge, c. Do we have the technology, or will it require R&D or special processes?

Using this decision tree, we created a rational workflow and were able to balance engineers' time, pricing, costing and resources between regular production and unusual requests.

If we can generalize this case, then evidently *the firm that wishes to be agile must have a planned system.* It will not only facilitate the work, but keep the product mix and profit levels aligned with strategic direction.

The Wikipedia article on Business Agility states: "agility should start from organizations' competitive bases and... mission, vision, and values"—distinctly strategic qualities!

> Out of all [25] tools included in the [Bain & Company] survey, 65 percent of respondents used strategic planning...second place behind the practice of benchmarking.
> ~Erika Olsen, *Strategic Planning for Dummies*

Management tools and techniques.

To conclude our review of internal business planning, here is a list of other tools and techniques, used either to support planning itself, or as solutions in specific circumstances:

High quality risk assessment. I designed HQRA to support the ERM initiative. It is a rigorous risk ID exercise. The uncertainties which typically escape one's attention in plans and projects can be identified and managed.

Environmental scan. ES (section 2.4) is the intelligence-gathering carried out in preparation for strategic planning.

Future scenarios planning. This is a technique to detect emerging trends and test strategic plan resiliency. It is the only way I have seen to plausibly discuss far future planning.

Stakeholder analysis. This is used for strategic planning (see section 2.5) and for major project risk assessment.

Logic model analysis. This is applied to operations conceived as repeatable processes, workflows, etc., (as discussed in section 3.2).

Principles of successful program implementation. Initiatives in all domains have high failure rates. Key success factors to incorporate into plans appear in the table in section 5.1.

Project management methodology. Project Management Institute and their methodology are the standard resources.

Performance management regime. Task completion by department or business unit is measured periodically by KPIs (key performance indicators) and tracked against planned targets.

Program evaluation. This specialized methodology is used in the public sector to verify the attainment of objectives and assess value-for-money.

Recap:
So far we have discussed internal organizational planning;

that is, the design of business functions, with a view to mature practice, even in early stages, to ensure scalability. We included a review of management disciplines and techniques (of course, to be used only selectively and instituted gradually) that shape the character of the firm.

To estimate progress towards mature practice for any aspect of the firm's management, use this model:

MANAGEMENT MATURITY MODEL

~based upon the Carnegie   Mellon Capability Maturity Model

5

OPTIMIZING and IMPROVING
Structured review of processes to introduce innovations / improvements.
Management & staff thinking is aligned with company goals and values.
Incremental improvements are detected and measured against goals.

4

MANAGED and MEASURED
Standard practices are consistently implemented and followed.
Quantitative measures – benchmarks for deliverables, times and cost –
in place to track performance. Predictable; permits accurate forecasting.

3

DEFINED PRACTICES
Standard practices are created, focusing on goals and quality criteria.
Practices are coordinated across the firm, guided by overall methodology.
Management is consistent, in principle, across departments.

2

REPEATABLE PRACTICES
Minimum discipline to repeat some processes, not analyzed/reviewed.
Mixed with random practice elsewhere in the firm.
Success is limited to projects of similar size/type.

1

INITIAL - AD HOC
Actions are taken on an as-needed basis, often responding to crisis.
Company atmosphere is unstable. Success depends on personalities.
Company over-commits; costs are uncontrolled and schedules overrun.

Figure 3. Management maturity model.

All this might prompt the reader to ask: why then is strategic planning even necessary? Cannot management maturity be reached without it? To answer, let's investigate what strategic planning consists of, and how it affects firm performance.

Strategic planning and firm performance.

In the academic and business literature, there are definite affirmations of strategic planning's positive effect on firm performance. Yet the matter is complicated by the definition of terms. The mere *appearance* of planning by creating pro forma documents is an empty exercise. At the same time, even well-researched documents cannot, by themselves, give results.

> If public leaders and managers find that a planning approach gets in the way of strategic thinking, acting, and learning, they should drop the approach and try a different one.
> ~John Byson, *Strategic Planning for Public and Non-profit Organizations*

Many researchers assert that planning involves mental processes, documents and action. One group recommends that we "recognize that strategic planning and its key dimensions represent a subtle and complex activity." Also: strategic planning "can serve as an integrating mechanism . . by building awareness or crystallizing consensus throughout the firm" (Glaister et al., 2008).

Strategic planning: definition.
Following this line of thinking, I define strategic planning as a complex interaction in the organization, comprising:

> a. the formal process steps (as outlined in this book) of research, discussion, writing and communicating;

> b. the understanding, unity of purpose and motivation developed in the minds of persons who follow these steps; and

> c. the translation of steps a. and b. into meaningful action.

Business failure rates are high. Those who chance upon a few best practices, or who accurately read the market and make decisions intuitively, can no doubt have some measure of success. Consequently, some reject planning as "too academic!" and act without research, discussion, or documentation.

In such cases, the trouble is that *the firm becomes dependent upon a dominant personality* who is, after all, neither omniscient, nor perfectly consistent, nor permanent. When this person becomes indisposed, leaves or behaves erratically, there is no capacity to make authoritative decisions.

Strategic planning must be built as a core competency of the firm.

The Why: the case for strategic planning.

Leaders who aspire to a world-class level of organizational development will want to build capacity. They want a management culture that is competent beyond one person's capricious influence. They also want an organization that is coherent—that has a sense of identity, defined aims, and consistent execution. Practitioners discover that strategic planning, in the form I describe it, is much more than the sum of its parts. It has a psychological effect, creating a shared vision and healthy interactions. This is the foundation of successful growth.

The three types of planning work together. *Strategic planning* enables employees to clarify in their own minds the organization's unique identity. They see how it fits into the broader landscape, and recognize their own roles. Mission, vision, values and goals cannot be realized unless documented and embraced by employees.

It follows that the *internal organizational plan* is not arbitrary, but designed to support definite strategic goals. *Operational plans,* in their turn, support clear objectives that move the firm in its desired direction.

> The kernel of a strategy contains three elements:
> a diagnosis, a guiding policy, and coherent action.
> ~Richard Rumelt, *Good Strategy/Bad Strategy*

Plan of this book.

The reader is now equipped with a solid rationale to validate the strategic planning initiative!

While this has been a long Introduction, it was necessary to clarify the three types of planning, and show the role of various management practices. These are all itemized in a table (next section): it is a generic planning and management schema. Use it as a reference.

In the following chapters we take several steps to prepare and create the strategic plan. Section 4 covers the role of the planning champion and how to facilitate the process.

In section 5 we review implementation success factors to make the crucial link between plans and action.

Finally, in section 6, we discuss strategic planning's specific beneficial effects on organizational culture.

1. Generic Planning and Management Schema

1.1 Schema

I INTERNAL ORGANIZATION PLANNING
a. Management team
TECHNIQUE: Planning practice: 3 types
b. Corporate governance, risk and compliance regime
TECHNIQUE: Information architectural planning
TECHNIQUE: Enterprise risk management (ERM)
c. Accounting and financial management
d. Business model: Method of engagement with market. Sales & marketing; communications/public relations.
e. Operations—Varied production and program areas
TECHNIQUE: Enterprise resource planning (ERP)
TECHNIQUE: Lean manufacturing; total quality management
TECHNIQUE: Quick response manufacturing
TECHNIQUE: Agile product development
TECHNIQUE: Knowledge management; organizational learning
f. Facilities and space planning
g. Design: Products; services; R&D; formal innovation program
h. ICT information and communications technology
i. HR policies: recruitment/retention; professional development
II STRATEGIC PLANNING: RESEARCH PHASE
1. Self-Identification: Unique assets and competencies
2. Mission
3. Values and Special Relationships
4. Environmental Scan
TECHNIQUE: Environmental scanning and future scenarios
5. Stakeholder Identification and Analysis
TECHNIQUE: Stakeholder identification and analysis tool
6. Capacity for Change
7. Vision
8. Gap Analysis

III STRATEGIC PLANNING: WRITING PHASE
1. Strategic goals
2. Objectives
IV OPERATIONAL PLANNING
1. Objectives
2. Tasks
3. Technical/administrative process, procedure, workflow
TECHNIQUE: Project management methodology
TECHNIQUE: High Quality Risk Assessment
TECHNIQUE: Logic model analysis
V EXECUTION PHASE
TECHNIQUE: Principles of successful program implementation
TECHNIQUE: Performance management regime
TECHNIQUE: Risk management [monitoring phase]
VI EVALUATION PHASE
Review and evaluation of programs and management systems.
TECHNIQUE: Performance management [review phase]
TECHNIQUE: Risk management [review phase]
TECHNIQUE: Program evaluation methodology

Figure 4. Generic organizational planning and management schema.

1.2 Explanation

The above schema (fig. 4) is a generic framework. It is not exhaustive; nor is it meant to be copied and followed slavishly. Of course, it would be impossible to implement everything listed. Its purpose is to put planning and management items in the right relative order. It gives a framework for you to compare with what you already have, and design your planning and management practice.

The three types of planning identified in the Introduction appear in this schema:

- internal organizational planning (Phase I)
- strategic planning (Phases II and III)
- operational planning (Phase IV)

Also, the optional management techniques discussed in the Introduction are shown in the list (in grey).

Although the steps are set in a notional order, in fact it will be necessary to use them, as I say, only selectively, and many of them iteratively.

Those interested in ERM and an extended discussion of successful program implementation (applicable to any kind of initiative) should see my *Solving the Enterprise Risk Management Puzzle* (2024).

We can now proceed to our main subject: the strategic planning process!

2. Strategic Planning: Research

The research phase for strategic planning is an exercise in information gathering, both internally (about the organization and its culture) and externally (about the surrounding economic and market conditions). This will serve as a basis for the team to formulate goals. We really have to "do the homework"; otherwise, the plan will necessarily be deficient. By contrast, fresh information will inspire confidence, as the work is more comprehensive.

Most of the work is best done in a series of facilitated group discussions, while certain aspects, notably the environmental scan and stakeholder analysis, require some research and writing. This duty can be shared among several people. This way the analysis is less likely to be skewed by one analyst's personal views, and the knowledge developed in the process is distributed. Researchers can collaborate to divide duties, create records and present their results.

(See section 4 for a discussion of roles and process.)

2.1 Self-Identification; Unique Competitive Advantage

In the first step of self-identification the team will begin by reflecting upon the qualities of the organization. The questions posed to the group are:

- What are our special assets and competencies?

- What sets us apart from the competition or (in the case of public sector organizations) parallel agencies in other jurisdictions?

Unique assets and competencies can be of many kinds; e.g., physical and tangible as well as intellectual, ethical, or relational. Certain organizations possess plant and equipment that is very difficult for others to duplicate; they could possess patents and other intellectual property; they may have personnel with highly specialized backgrounds.

The unique aspect may not be a feature of the product, but rather, a certain combination of products and services—for example, extraordinary customer care as part of a manufacturing operation. It could be well-developed institutional connections that give access to special skills. It might be detection and agility, whereby the firm, thanks to its relationships with clients, discovers their needs and fulfills them within a comparatively short time-to-market. Peter Senge, expert on organizational learning, said in this regard: "The ability to learn faster than your competitors may be the only sustainable competitive advantage." For an arts group, it could be the ability to give the most acclaimed interpretation of a given artistic form, composer, or playwright.

Develop a list of special assets, with a view to narrowing down the selection to the one (or the combination) that is not only difficult to copy, but *the most highly valued aspect of the business*. This is the unique competitive advantage

(UCA). The table below (fig. 5) sets out categories to help identify unique assets, and shows how they confer value.

SOURCE OF SPECIAL ASSET	
A. PERSONNEL Intellectual capacity Manual/technical skill Formal qualifications Social and communications skills Experience Contacts and relationships	**B. MATERIAL and RESOURCES** Raw materials; resources Information and data Facilities and infrastructure Geographic location Equipment Financial
C. PROCESS, PROCEDURE OR METHOD Technical Industrial Administrative Social Artistic	**D. INSTITUTIONAL** Legal, regulatory Political Contractual Ethical; moral; philosophical Historical
E. COMBINATION of elements from A, B, C, D.	

TYPES OF VALUE OF SPECIAL ASSET
Cost Quality Timeliness Efficiency (lower inputs for a given output; quality constant) Effectiveness in view of end goal Power; Influence Reliability; Performance Depth; Sophistication; Variety; Complexity Exclusivity; Reputation; Prestige; Suitability; Appeal

Figure 5. Special assets: sources and type of value.

The purpose of this exercise is to discover and define the UCA (if not already done), bring it to light, and acknowledge its central place in subsequent planning.

This exercise imparts a sense of identity. People generally want to be associated with something that is somehow exclusive and privileged. While a mission statement (discussed next) expresses a cause that is greater than the individual, the UCA enables people to feel that they are carrying out that mission *in a way that no one else can.* This is a source of pride and loyalty to the firm. Planners should safeguard and celebrate this special competency.

The Wikipedia author quoted above cautions us, "Agile enterprises do not adhere to the concept of sustained competitive advantage" and yet insists that "organizational agility should start from the organization's competitive bases." My interpretation is that the UCA is not an ephemeral selling point, but a continual source of innovation and value.

This raises the point: the UCA might be in danger of becoming irrelevant. The planning team must ask:

1. Is our current unique competitive advantage a sufficient source of long-term differentiation for the firm?

2. Will the organization rest content with its current level of innovation, learning, research and development—or should we seek to increase our capacity in these areas?

2.2 Mission

The mission statement is a one or two sentence expression. It answers the question, "What is our purpose?" It is a declaration of the organization's most essential concern.

> Mission statements need to be remembered.
> Make yours clear, concise, and direct.
> ~Heyden Enochson, onstrategyhq.com

Do not include in your mission statement things that are subject to changeable conditions. Also, avoid using hyperbole ("the best," the most efficient,") etc., as it is vague.

Rather, describe the core activity; the reason for the firm's existence. The mission could be not only to make good products, but also "to educate, guide, and problem-solve."

The mission statement—typically displayed on the wall and used in marketing materials—is not only used internally, but is also public-facing. *Clients will immediately compare their own experience with the mission statement.* It therefore becomes a tool for accountability.

A single, well-crafted and memorable phrase helps to unify the attitude of employees by expressing a high ideal. The table below shows examples that express a compelling purpose; focus on the needs of the client; speak to the public; inspire staff motivation; and have a perennial quality.

MISSION STATEMENTS—EXAMPLES

FIRM—MISSION STATEMENT	REMARKS
Advance Auto Parts. To provide personal vehicle owners and enthusiasts with the vehicle related products and knowledge that fulfill their wants and needs at the right price. Our friendly, knowledgeable and professional staff will help inspire, educate and problem-solve for our customers.	Balanced for clients and employees. Specific, not vague.
American Financial Group. Our purpose is to enable individuals and businesses to manage financial risk. We provide insurance products and services tailored to meet the specific and ever-changing financial risk exposures facing our customers. We build value for our investors through the strength of our customers' satisfaction and by consistently producing superior operating results.	Perennial quality expressed in "ever-changing financial risk exposures."
AmerisourceBergen. To build shareholder value by delivering pharmaceutical and healthcare products, services and solutions in innovative and cost-effective ways. We will realize this mission by setting the highest standards in service, reliability, safety and cost containment in our industry.	"Highest standards" may be hard to prove or live up to.
The Bank of New York. We strive to be the acknowledged global leader and preferred partner in helping our clients succeed in the world's rapidly evolving financial markets.	Simple; avoids hyperbole.
Erie Insurance Group. To provide our policyholders with as near perfect protection, as near perfect service as is humanly possible and to do so at the lowest possible cost.	Interesting standards; demanding.
Darden Restaurant. To nourish and delight everyone we serve.	Brevity is memorable.

Figure 6. Mission statements—examples with remarks.

2.3 Values and Special Relationships

Corporate values can be most usefully defined as principles that guide the behaviour of the organization's personnel and their relationships with stakeholders. They may be single words or phrases; but their intended meaning should be spelled out. (See fig. 7 for examples.)

Values, in the sense that I have described, are underrated, because they have more economic value and carry more risk than is often supposed. Their true significance is in how they are operationalized.

I once facilitated a session with a government agency in charge of land use licensing. They were experiencing negative feedback from clients. After an hour of discussion, it seemed the mechanics of the program were fine—I was puzzled. But all the real problems came to light when we started to examine *values*, such as timeliness, transparency, fairness, consistency in outcomes of decisions, etc.

Corporate, organizational, or professional values must be defined as part of the planning exercise. Their source may be obvious (such as a professional code or standard in a regulated industry) or may be derived from rules of customer care, a philosophy, or an ethical standard. Values may be closely bound up with a particular client group.

Finally, be mindful that a facilitated session, where employees define their own values and create their own code of conduct, has a positive effect on staff morale.

CORPORATE VALUES—EXAMPLES

These examples, with brief explanations, meet the definition of *principles guiding the behaviour of the organization's personnel.*

VALUE	REMARKS
Integrity = moral consistency	After the Golden Rule, probably *the* central value
Transparency = openness in decision-making	Classic in good governance
Accountability = responsibility for the use of resources in light of promised results	Classic in good governance
Fairness = lack of prejudice or favouritism in the rendering of service	Classic in good service
Safety first = putting human welfare ahead of the demands of operations	Classic in industry and high-risk vocations
Lead by example = take personal responsibility to follow rules and enact values	Discourages hypocrisy
Timeliness = minimum time to render service	Shows respect for clients
Be your own customer (SquareSpace) = deliver results that you would gladly accept	Practical way to think about quality
Seek diverse perspectives (Twitter) = bring different types of expertise to problems	Difficult problems yield to multidisciplinary approach
Take risk-optimized decisions = take risks to an extent consistent with company guidelines and values	Strikes a good balance between extreme risk aversion and mere recklessness
Empathy = put oneself in another's position	Leads to increased understanding of co-workers' and clients' difficulties

Figure 7. Values—examples with remarks.

33

2.4 Environmental Scan

At this point, we have defined sufficiently the nature of the organization itself—who we are, and what our purpose is. Now it is time to look at the wider world.

The environmental scan asks the following questions:

- What are the general conditions and trends—locally, nationally and globally—that affect our organization and our mission?
- What developments and innovations are taking place in our industry/profession/sector among competitors and in other jurisdictions?
- Which of our major stakeholders' key challenges can we help solve?

To make the environmental scan feasible, but also incisive and insightful, assign the task to talented in-house analysts. They can use web, scholarly, expert blog and trade publication sources; conference proceedings; and interviews with internal experts and consultants. This retains within the firm the tacit, incidental and implicit knowledge gained.

> Processes that render good companies incapable of responding to change are often those that define *how market research is habitually done.*
> ~Clayton Christensen, *The Innovator's Dilemma*

The research analysts must divide up their search topics, coordinate their work, and present results to the planning team. They can use a multi-media format including text, graphics, and video; tell stories, and describe scenarios. This will engage people with different learning styles.

The environmental scan can also be targeted internally, within the firm itself, especially if it is a large and complex organization. Normally the report has two components:

1. PESTLE Scan. This is a general report on conditions, trends and forecasts under the headings: Political; Economic; Social; Technological; Legal; Environmental that spells out the implications for the industry.

2. Industry, sector, or professional environment. The purpose of this component is to discover (if you haven't already) the next "big wave" in your field. What are the most innovative practices that could disrupt the whole industry, whether in technology, market, products, delivery model, customer relationship, etc.? What are the related industries where the firm's special abilities can be used?

What I have found in this type of discussion is that there is much more tacit knowledge in the firm than you had probably imagined. This is a chance to capture it. What is more, the competition is likely not doing this systematically.

Whatever the innovative practices are in your field, _chart a path for your organization to be a top practitioner and thought leader_. To get started, see figure 8.

ENVIRONMENTAL SCAN ELEMENTS

What macro trends are most relevant to your organization?

Political / Governmental / Legal
Federal government programs; political agendas and support
Relative federal-state/provincial-municipal powers and funding
Regulation and controls; private ownership/delivery of public services
Case law; precedents; legal risk

Economic
Central and international banking; global governance institutions
Financial markets; currencies; blockchain technology; cryptocurrencies
Commodities; precious/industrial metals; food production
Real property; intellectual property; intellectual capital; productivity
International imports/exports and trade balances
Interest rates; exchange rates; inflation/deflation/stagflation
Debt/savings - household/corporate/government; credit availability and default
Employment; prices; wages/salaries; income disparities; taxation
Commercial trends; entertainment, (il)legal substances, repo, debt consolidation

Social
Global demographics; work force demographics
Civil organizations, trends, activism and movements

Technological
Renewable energy; hydro; petroleum/natural gas; coal; nuclear
Plant and equipment; electronics; micro and nano technology
Information technology, interconnectivity, AI and IoT
Security tech - biometrics; surveillance; RFID

Environmental
Natural disaster; degradation; disappearance of arable land; air quality
Internal/ambient conditions of facilities

Which trends influence your sector/ industry/ profession?
Developments and interests of key stakeholders
Developments in your supply chain industries
Trends in your industry or area of specialization
Events within competition and peers
Solutions used in other jurisdictions

What are your authoritative / deep sources?
Thought leaders| Blogs| Contacts| Industry/trade journals| Innovation sources|
Books| Professional associations| Scholarly articles| Awards/citations| Standards

Figure 8. Environmental scan elements.

2.5 Stakeholder Analysis

The world of stakeholders (also known as the "task environment") is the sphere within which your organization interacts, that is, clients, customers, program beneficiaries, supply chain, regulators, etc. We want to ask:

- What are the entities that we interact with?
- What are their motives and interests?
- What is the nature of their connection to the firm?
- What is their relative degree of power and influence?

As shown in figure 9, take these steps: First, list the stakeholders. Then, define the mutual obligations and interactions between each entity and your organization, including contractual dependencies. Summarize the interests or motive of the entities, as well as the degrees of influence and power they have. Assess even their legitimacy, if appropriate. Create a matrix to record this information. This will permit an estimate of the *criticality of the relationship*, shown in the diagram as low, medium or high.

To complete the analysis, write a description of the paramount concerns of critical stakeholders and nascent trends affecting them. (There will likely be overlap with the environmental scan.) As a result, you will identify the most important stakeholder issues to be addressed later in the strategic plan's statement of goals and objectives. If feasible, get stakeholder reps to help with this last part. As long as the input is balanced, your analysis will be better informed.

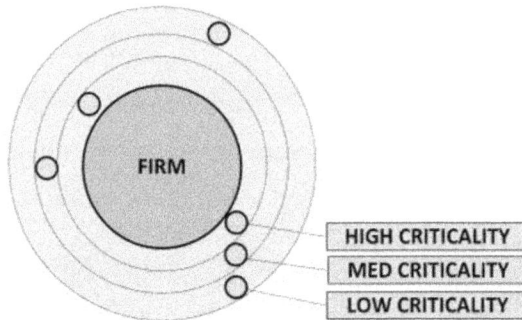

1. IDENTIFY STAKEHOLDERS	2. CREATE PROFILE FOR EACH	3. DETERMINE RESULTANT SCORE
...in the "task environment"; i.e., the network of entities with which the organization regularly interacts.	(a) Obligations; Dependencies (b) Interaction; Deliverables (c) Interests; Motives; and Goals (d) Degrees of Power/ Influence (e) Degree of Legitimacy	Mark each stakeholder on diagram according to degree of criticality = low /med/ high or use numerical scale.

Figure 9. Stakeholder analysis.

2.6 Capacity for Change

To plan and execute fresh initiatives, you need to know: What is the degree of openness and ability among employees to accept and enact change, improvements and new methods? If the stakeholder analysis above was at all inward-looking, then you have begun to consider this.

The organizational culture may be entrenched; it might be rooted in engrained habits and attitudes. Another possibility is that employees have "change fatigue," because a series of poorly conceived programs has had no meaningful effect.

Organizational change cannot occur without the consent and willing participation of those concerned. One of the best ways to achieve this is to involve personnel in the creative process. People are more likely to support plans which they themselves have helped build. Besides developing a sense of ownership of plans, they have the chance to prove to themselves that the process is beneficial.

As you explore avenues for change, you will identify training needs. The organization's learning and working styles have to be assessed. Some employees will be better disposed to creating written materials; others will require a hands-on, tactile and visual approach using physical artifacts, signage, tools and equipment.

Take account of the culture, and be mindful of the capacity and appetite for change as you hold planning discussions. Essentially, we want to avoid being blindsided by the most common reasons for program failure, and make use of success factors (explained in more detail in section 5).

In an initial strategic planning session I led, it was capacity for change that the General Manager insisted on as the first item for discussion. He described a prevailing attitude among shop floor staff of indifference or negativity towards creative efforts. His solution? He organized an excursion for them to tour facilities that had already gone through a Lean Manufacturing transformation—the first educational effort of its kind in the company's history. The staff were amazed by what they saw, and took photos for their own work plan.

2.7 Vision

By the time this stage is reached, the planning team understands much better than it did at the outset the essential nature of the organization: its unique characteristics, purpose, and values. The team members realize more clearly that the firm does not operate in a vacuum—they see the economic and industry context, important trends, conditions, and opportunities, including the concerns of major stakeholders. They also have an idea of the employee culture and its predisposition to change.

The facilitator can now realistically expect a fully informed answer to these crucial questions: Where is the organization going? What is our vision for the desired future state of the organization? Set the time frame for one to two years.

The "vision" is just that: an image or picture in one's mind, although translated into words (maybe supplemented by graphics, see next page). It does not describe the path to reach the ideal future state. That path is a series of actions to be stated later.

The vision describes, instead, an ideal state of affairs where the organization's goals are already attained. Participants should contribute their descriptions addressing areas such as: realization of the mission; utilization of unique assets; new products, services or business model; an innovation program up and running; and benefits accruing to clients. The vision is—in a sense—fanciful; but a plausible and vitally necessary picture, grounded in the analysis done in previous sections.

This visualizing exercise engages the planners' imaginations, and allows a full expression of their intended creative work.

Someone may declare a future scene that captures everything in one inspired view. The best example I have seen is the idea of a "Wow!" company—an organization that is so well organized, innovative, and impressive that anyone who visits its offices, sees its products, or walks onto the shop floor, will stop and exclaim "Wow!"

As long as coherent plans and implementation efforts support the idea, it can be turned into a reality. That is the emotive and transformative potential of an inspiring vision!

The image below is a sample (single) infographic. When developed in a series, its power lies in a particularly effective combination of images with text, appealing to a broad audience. A company vision could be conveyed like that.

Visuals are a universal language, so what better way to show the world your company's vision than by using infographics?

Courtesy www.easel.ly

Figure 10. Infographic.

2.8 Strategic Identity

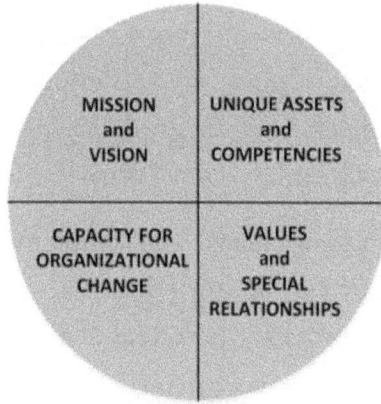

MISSION and VISION	UNIQUE ASSETS and COMPETENCIES
CAPACITY FOR ORGANIZATIONAL CHANGE	VALUES and SPECIAL RELATIONSHIPS

STRATEGIC IDENTITY DIAGRAM

Figure 11. Strategic identity.

Now that at a trial version of the vision is done, the planners can assemble what I call Strategic Identity.

The diagram in figure 11 is a comprehensive expression of the character and broad aims of the organization. It can be accompanied by a one-page written summation of each quadrant, drawing upon the activities completed. It is the culmination of the research effort. While mission and vision are included, the goals and objectives do not appear, because specific actions to pursue the vision can change.

The significance of the Strategic Identity diagram is that it helps planners to focus mentally on all that is *truly essential* and *relatively enduring* about the organization.

2.9 Gap Analysis

Gap analysis is a transitional step from the research to the writing phase, where planners will actually formulate strategic goals and objectives.

Gap analysis systematically compares the Vision with the organization's current status. Consequently, it is a sober realization of the distance or gap between the present state of development of the firm and the desired future state. It is just here, where the vision can be reaffirmed and adjusted to suit closer possibilities.

A complementary approach is to carry out "SWOT," i.e., to list Strengths, Weaknesses, Opportunities, and Threats that have become apparent in the study, so far. (Naming "Threats" should not be construed as risk assessment, which is a structured investigation of the uncertainty associated with planned objectives.) "Threats", rather, are trends or conditions that will tend to undermine the mission.

The team is now ready to start writing the strategic goals and objectives. It stands to reason that it can do so only now, after having "done its homework" so thoroughly in the previous steps. A strategic plan that is comprehensive and well-informed is bound to inspire confidence.

3. Strategic Planning: Writing

3.1 Formulate Strategic Goals

Thanks to the work done in the Research Phase, all of the raw material is now at hand to create the strategic goals. However, there will have to be a certain amount of interpretive work to properly select and formulate the goals, and set them in order of priority. It helps to get input from all the team members to arrive at a consensus.

Begin by reviewing together the main conclusions of the environmental scan about critical trends and issues, as well as the identified opportunities to innovate, become a practice and thought leader, add value, and serve client groups. Next, recall the elements of Strategic Identity, and focus on the vision statement. Finally, review the gap analysis, and take a realistic view of the capacity for change.

With all of the foregoing freshly recalled, set a time frame of one to two years. Try to select and formulate the strategic goals. Participants in the planning session will likely gravitate towards a few obvious candidates for important goals. Of course, simply maintaining current operations does not constitute a strategic plan! Meaningful strategic goals incorporate new challenges. Forward motion keeps the organization viable.

Goals have either an external or an internal orientation. Externally oriented goals engage with the task environment in a new way (new products, markets, institutional connections, etc.). Internally oriented goals (as discussed in the Introduction) are concerned with major undertakings to build and improve the organization's systems and methods, transform its business model, or increase its capacity.

> The same idea, product, service, or technology may fail with one business model and succeed with another.
> ~Benson Garner, blog.strategyzer.com

A merger or acquisition is an example of an internally oriented goal, in the sense that it modifies the firm itself.
Goal statements must describe the end result—what you want to achieve. Notice one important thing, which, in my

experience, is by far the most common mistake planners make: the goals (although inspired by a vision) must not be vaguely expressed. As in the Wow inspiration, you must associate the end effect with defined accomplishments.

For example, if the goal were to create an online store, it would not be advisable to state: "Build the best e-commerce website in the industry," simply because no one knows what that really means. It would be much more useful to formulate the goal as follows: "Build an e-commerce website that is fully functional and reliable, to the following specifications." Then, *list the minimum required technical and quality criteria.*

It is helpful to do an internet search on "SMART" goals and review their characteristics, along these lines: Specific (in their formulation, as illustrated above); Measurable (or at least tangible or demonstrable); Agreed-upon (thanks to the consensus approach); Realistic (technically feasible, with available resources); and Time-bound (on a schedule).

A strategic goal is sometimes quickly conceived as a target, such as "Increase revenues by fifteen percent." New production targets or profit levels are, of course, worthwhile. But that sort of goal should be expressed in term of new activities to make it feasible (such as using better methods aimed at improved efficiencies). The actions needed to reach the goal should be planned and coordinated.

By contrast, if the goal is stated only as a number with no context, then people will be left to "manage to the numbers," i.e., to reach the goal (in this case fifteen percent increased revenues) without regard for the effects upon the other aspects of the business, such as lead time, quality, or customer service.

As previously discussed, an important internal change initiative could be formulated as a strategic goal. This could be a new management regime such as Lean Manufacturing or Enterprise Risk Management; or a systems application for Enterprise Resource Planning.

In the strategic plan, there should be at least two strategic goals. Perhaps three would be ideal; but more than four or five might be unmanageable. In any case, it is inadvisable to pursue simultaneously more than one goal oriented to *internal* change.

3.2 Objectives, Projects, Workflows, Strat Plan Facsimile

Objectives. An objective is a subset of a strategic goal that is written into the strategic plan, and then typically undertaken within an operational unit or department.

The objectives supporting any particular corporate strategic goal are milestones along a path towards the goal, that is, the subsidiary accomplishments by a branch, department or business unit, expressed as deliverables on a time-line.

Objectives can be conceptualized as ordered items. Take the above example of an e-commerce website. The statement of this strategic goal, with its associated objectives, might be recorded in the form of a chart or table (see fig. 12).

The example below is simplified. To be complete, the quality specifications or criteria would have to be listed, i.e., the minimum requirements to achieve the expected goal. Also, the timeline is artificial (certain things can actually run concurrently).

But, for the sake of illustration: the HR and Finance departments are shown to be responsible for specific deliverables.

The IT department itself is responsible for objectives 1.2 and 1.4—and for coordinating the completed goal.

GOAL 1 E-COMMERCE WEBSITE—Lead Responsible: IT DEPT.			
Build a fully developed, functional and reliable website using noted criteria:			

OBJECTIVE	CRITERIA	LEAD RESPONSI- BLE	DEAD- LINE DATE
1.1 Hire contractors.	List of roles / qualifications: (...) (...) (...)	HR DEPT	15 Feb
1.2 Sign ISP contract. (Internet Service Provider)	List of contract clauses: (...) (...) (...)	IT DEPT	15 Mar
1.3 Web design.	List of features/functions: (...) (...) (...)	FINANCE	15 Apr
1.4 Testing and Commissioning	List of commissioning steps: (...) (...) (...)	IT DEPT	15 May

Figure 12. Example: Strategic goal and associated operational objectives.

Projects. The operational objectives can be complex, so they are broken down into steps by the branch or department concerned. In fact, these subject–matter experts

49

will likely further define the quality criteria. It is perfectly feasible to use formal project management methodology to execute operational objectives.

The factors that distinguish a formal project from a perennial activity are the project's exceptional or temporary nature, and its defined limits of scope and duration.

PM methodology is a disciplined way to track intended accomplishments: resources (personnel and budget), schedule, critical path, and deliverables. It is used at the highest level—to manage the strategic plan itself and track goals—as well as at the department levels.

Here is a recap of the planning of goals and objectives:

a. *The strategic plan*, expressed as goals, informs operational plans, expressed as objectives. The strategic planning document itself lists both the goals and objectives, each with its specifications and timeline.

b. *The operational plan* of the business unit or department lists the objectives they have received and are responsible for. They can develop further quality criteria (as they have the required expertise) and must manage execution, likely using project management methodology.

The project manager can decide the granularity of work breakdown described in a project plan. The use of terminology (e.g., "goal," "objective," "task") must be consistent. This preserves the principle of alignment, whereby lower orders of activity support (as directly as possible) corporate-level strategic aims.

Workflows. Instead of hierarchical activities, operations can take the form of a repeatable process that is established as a permanent activity (e.g., a process for insurance claims, licensing, or other administrative purpose; or a technical procedure such as the steps in a medical testing laboratory or manufacturing facility).

These can often best be described by a graphic: a flowchart, workflow diagram, or "logic model" (see fig. 13). Operational plans can either envisage the creation of such a process, or undertake to optimize an existing one.

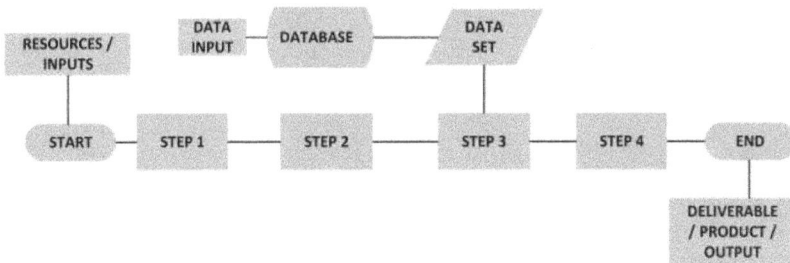

Figure 13. Flowchart or workflow diagram.

Strategic plan facsimile. Now that strategic goals and operational objectives are completed (even in draft) let us look at the format of the strategic planning document. Figure 14 shows both a Table of Contents and a Goal Sheet as templates. It is not only a plan, but a management tool, with columns for updating at periodic meetings. The background work (environmental scan, etc.) for the plan should be attached for reference in a series of appendices.

STRATEGIC PLAN		
DOC VERSION:	DATE:	
DOC OWNER:	FILE:	
CONTACT:		
DISTRIBUTION LIST:		

TABLE OF CONTENTS	
ITEM	**PAGE**
INTRODUCTION; PARTICIPANTS; PROCESS	----
GOAL 1	----
OBJECTIVE 1.1	----
OBJECTIVE 1.2	----
OBJECTIVE 1.3	----
GOAL 2	
OBJECTIVE 2.1	----
OBJECTIVE 2.2	----
OBJECTIVE 2.3	----
GOAL 3	
OBJECTIVE 3.1	----
OBJECTIVE 3.2	----
OBJECTIVE 3.3	----
OBJECTIVE 3.4	----
APPENDICES	
01 SELF–IDENTIFICATION; UNIQUE COMPETITIVE ADVANTAGE	----
02 MISSION	----
03 VALUES AND SPECIAL RELATIONSHIPS	----
04 ENVIRONMENTAL SCAN	----
05 STAKEHOLDER ANALYSIS	----
06 CAPACITY FOR CHANGE	----
07 VISION	----
08 STRATEGIC IDENTITY	----
09 GAP ANALYSIS	----

Figure 14. Strategic plan document—facsimile—1.

STRATEGIC GOAL 1	LEAD	DUE DATE	STATUS	REMARKS
UPDATE : MM DD YY				
STATEMENT:				

FEATURES: FUNCTIONS - ESSENTIAL	QUALITY CRITERIA
☐	
☐	
☐	
☐	
☐	

FEATURES; FUNCTIONS - NON-ESSENTIAL	
☐	
☐	
☐	
☐	
☐	

OPERATIONAL OBJECTIVES	LEAD	DUE DATE	STATUS	REMARKS
OBJECTIVE 1.1				
STATEMENT:				

OBJECTIVE 1.2				
STATEMENT:				

OBJECTIVE 1.3				
STATEMENT:				

TIME LINE

OBJECTIVE 1.1				
	OBJECTIVE 1.1			
		OBJECTIVE 1.1		
JAN	FEB	MAR	APR	MAY

Figure 14. Strategic plan document—facsimile—2.

4. Facilitating the Process

4.1 Planning Champion; Key Roles; Facilitated Session

Planning champion. One person is likely to be designated the "champion" of the strategic planning process. This person must not only organize the materials and set the meetings, but also help select the participants, facilitate the discussion, and create the documents. It is feasible for two persons to share the role of champion. Organizational ability, as well as analytical and facilitation skills, are paramount.

The champion may be responsible for conducting the environmental scan and other research, or may be able to delegate that role. As mentioned, if research is outsourced to a consultancy, the disadvantage is that tacit knowledge developed will not be retained within the organization. Also, consulting firms will sometimes just give a list of generic industry issues, rather than develop an environmental scan finely tuned to the organization's needs.

Key roles. The strategic planning team itself will normally consist of people at the senior management level. An executive sponsor must help the champion by giving official sanction to the planning initiative, and by ensuring the champion has sufficient resources and authority to call meetings. Stakeholders—such as industry or regulatory experts, client groups, or program beneficiaries—should, where possible, take an advisory role. Internal stakeholders include staff, managers, the executive, and board of directors. Representatives can review drafts of the plan.

The mode of sharing information and eliciting comments must be carefully managed if there is risk of inappropriate disclosure of sensitive information. It is a matter of striking a balance. Up to a certain point, planners will want to work in secret; yet, later consultation with stakeholders ensures a robust and widely supported plan.

Facilitated session. Round table facilitated sessions help build a common understanding among subject matter experts. By contrast, when doing individual interviews or sending out surveys, I have found that respondents can have highly varied ideas of definitions, purpose and scope. The resulting mass of data cannot be easily aggregated.

The champion(s) must have sufficient confidence to facilitate group discussion, and simultaneously take notes and lead participants to consensus. I recommend, especially if the material is highly sensitive or contentious, that champions get formal training in facilitation.

At a minimum, the facilitator should be able to chair a meeting, interpret participants' comments and synthesize them into a draft plan. The facilitator will normally use a projector, so that meeting participants can follow the line-by-line entries, and make corrections where needed.

About five or six participants is ideal for facilitated sessions. The discussion is too insular with fewer people; with more, the process becomes somewhat unwieldy. The facilitator must elicit input from all participants and not let any one person dominate the discussion.

I have often used a train-the-trainer or transfer-of-skills model. Acting as champion and lead facilitator, I usually assist departmental managers or analysts by demonstrating the process, then encouraging them to run their own operational planning sessions and integrate the review of plans into regular meetings.

5. Link to Successful Operations

5.1 Success Factors for Execution

Do comprehensive and well-informed strategic and operational plans lead, necessarily, to successful execution? Unfortunately, no. Many planners and managers suffer the "implementation gap," attested to by the high failure rate and chronic under-delivery of management initiatives in all fields. What is usually lacking in failed attempts at execution is an understanding of motivational factors and the perennial dynamics of new programs. Pay attention to the common reasons for program failure and be sure to build into your plans the corresponding principles of program success. See figure 15.

Link to Successful Operations

CAUSE OF PROGRAM FAILURE	PRINCIPLE OF PROGRAM SUCCESS

01 PROGRAM GOALS and MANAGEMENT DIRECTION

Goals of the new program are poorly defined, or—even with well formulated goals—management veers away from them because priorities are inconsistent, management is fickle, and the company too often changes direction.	**Program has well-conceived SMART goals,** initially oriented to demonstrable results of pilot projects, and focused on a definite value proposition. Management is determined to persist in the initiative as a progressive aim.

02 SENIOR EXECUTIVE SUPPORT

Support from the executive or senior management is ineffectual: it may be sporadic or superficial (just lip-service), or just nominal, without substance.	**Senior management and executive actively engage** in the new initiative, demand real deliverables and then review and give feedback, showing genuine participation.

03 STAFF SUPPORT

Staff is indifferent, shows profound lack of interest, or outright rejection of the new program. They feel it is an imposition that is unrelated to their daily work.	**The new program must answer the actual needs of staff.** They participate in the design of the initiative, which must help solve their business problems. Staff buy-in is secured as they gain a sense of value and ownership.

04 CAUSAL MODEL

The new initiative is wrongly conceived, based on a misidentified root problem or a faulty idea of its cause.	**The causality is explored and demonstrated** in pilot projects or trials where the mechanism causing the problem is confirmed.

05 PROGRAM PRACTICALITY

The initiative appears ill-suited to the organization because it does not address its needs, meet its goals, observe its values, give financial value, or show cultural appropriateness.	**The initiative addresses the real work** and is adapted to the organizational culture. It focuses on improved quality of results, clarity on enactment of values, efficiencies, and novel solutions.

06 IMPLEMENTATION STYLE

Blanket or monolithic program implementation imposes unrealistic demands; it provokes resistance, as staff are overwhelmed.	**Incremental or phased implementation**: permits iterative refinement of methods by end users; gradual ownership and acceptance.

07 PROGRAM PROMOTION

Promotional events and promises are given in advance of proving the concept, which entails a high risk of failure and reputational damage.	**Celebration of small successes** in trial projects, with demonstrable benefits, builds practitioners' confidence.

08 PROGRAM RESOURCING	
A poorly resourced program shows that the champion is not prepared to help staff and that senior management is not serious.	**Tools, templates and training** are available on demand. White papers, case studies and other artifacts serve as proof-of-concept.
09 RELATION TO EXISTING PRACTICE	
The initiative is an administrative burden; staff cannot keep up with the extra work imposed by new methods.	**The new program, while requiring work up front, eventually integrates** well with management practice and makes it efficient.
10 PROGRAM CHAMPION	
The new initiative does not have a home or a spearhead, causing multiple interpretations, loss of direction, and ultimate failure.	**The new program, initiative, operation, or policy has a champion** to communicate concepts, unify language, set up resources, and build capacity through facilitation.

Figure 15. Causes of program failure and associated principles of success.

> Bridging the gap between strategy and execution
> is difficult... OKRs align team and individual
> goals with a company's strategic plan.
> ~MIT Sloan Mgt Review on John Doerr,
> *Measuring What Matters*

6. Effects of Planning on the Organization

6.1 Team Building; Culture; Accountability

Team building. We cannot imagine that documented plans, by themselves, even if informed by the principles of successful program implementation, will automatically lead to organizational change. The studies on strategic planning discussed in the Introduction show an important emphasis on the *interactive aspects* of the entire exercise.

Participants in strategic planning will discover that the exercise itself—the background work, extended discussion, and documentation—is revelatory, and creates a change in attitude. Perhaps for the first time in the firm's history, the senior management team is obliged to think through the logic of the firm's existence, and articulate its identity. The collective psychological effect benefits the organization.

I once led a contentious project planning session with private interests and government agencies with hopelessly antagonistic mandates and values. Health advocates were fighting against powerful industry groups. I found the best approach was to focus on their ostensible common project aims. The rigour of the approach to define a joint purpose saved the day: the participants finished with a shared vision—and even remained together after I left to manage the project as a cohesive team.

Culture. This raises the question: how does the planning process affect employees and their culture, beyond the planning team itself? According to the principles of knowledge management, the strategic planning process should involve consultation with employees, and distribution of documentation in multiple formats and channels. (Whether to share certain materials regarded as confidential will be a separate decision.)

Consultation can be carried out through surveys and events such as "all-hands meetings," organized periodically during the planning process. The idea is to elicit employee feedback on draft plans; invite questions, comments and suggestions; review the mission statement; discuss how to operationalize values; and celebrate progress. Such meetings then become a regular practice: they give employees a share of participation and control in company direction. The crucial point: if carried out in a genuine manner, these interactions build trust between management and staff. Note also that the use of new language inspires new thinking and behaviours.

Such dialogue builds cooperation and so makes it easier to establish, for example, a compensation and rewards regime. A system built on common ground will be transparent, fair, and commensurate with productivity.

Accountability. Accountability is responsibility, whether towards oneself, employees, peers, or superiors, for promised results. How does planning enable accountability?

Once established, the strategic identity should undergo revision only infrequently. Therefore, the mission and vision (relatively enduring aspects) provide a stable standard of accountability for checking the firm's overall progress.

Operational plans are management tools. A review at regular meetings of due dates, deliverables, and status constitutes an accountability framework, whether at the corporate or departmental level. Frequent stand-up meetings among peers, as long as they are kept lively by focusing on exceptions reporting, build a sense of continuous mutual accountability.

When the firm's work is conceived in such a highly organized way, it raises morale. People start to feel that the business is well in hand, while each individual's role and contributions are clear. Accountability is then integrated with the business and less a matter of superficial compliance.

Conclusion

At the outset, I emphasized the importance for readers/practitioners to interpret their own organizational contexts and apply generic principles. Let's review important ones:

1. Strategic planning is not an informal discussion, nor just the documents. It is a structured and interactive process, and distinct from other types of planning and management techniques. It has a positive effect on firm performance.

2. The strategic identity of the firm, including unique competencies, vision and mission, is closely tied to each employee's self-concept and sense of motivation.

3. Capacity for organizational change, as well as employee culture and learning styles, must be accounted for when initiating a strategic planning practice.

4. Newly created plans, in all domains, will suffer from an implementation gap, and can founder in roll-out for several reasons. It is necessary to build in principles of successful program implementation.

5. Planning aligns the continuing daily business with overall strategy, and enables the management of accountability.

6. A subtle effect of the strategic planning discipline is a collective psychological benefit that gives resilience to the organization.

In conclusion, leaders who want their organization to reach its potential must strive to attain mature methods and culture. I have shown that strategic planning establishes the foundation. The background research, articulation of identity and goals, and engagement of personnel all prepare the organization to meet the demands of growth and become pre-eminent in its field.

References

Baker, W. H. et al. (1993) "Business planning in successful small firms." *Long Range Planning* Vol. 26, 6

CB Insights (2018) "The top 20 reasons startups fail" cbinsights.com

Collins, Jim (2001) *Good to Great,* Harper Business.

Glaister, K. W. et al. (2008) "A causal analysis of formal strategic planning and firm performance" *Management Decision* Vol.46, 3

Kelly, Alan (2015) "Does Agile work outside software?" agileconnection.com

Lewis, Robin "Amazon -- The "Rock And A Hard Place" For Third-Party Merchants." 21 January, 2016. Forbes.

Lussier, Robert N. (1996) "Reasons why small businesses fail" *The Entrepreneurial Executive* Vol. 1, 2

Miller, C.; Cardinal, L. (1994) "Strategic planning and firm performance" *Academy of Management Journal* Vol. 37, 6

Mission statements.com Examples from Fortune 500 companies.

Robertson, Edward (2024) *Solving the Enterprise Risk Management Puzzle: Secrets to Successful Implementation.* Amazon.

Robinson, R. B.; Pearce, J. A. (1983) "The impact of formalized strategic planning on financial performance in small organizations." *Strategic Management Journal* Vol. 4

Schwenk, C. R.; Shrader, C. B. (1993) "Effects of formal strategic planning on financial performance in small firms: a meta-analysis." *Entrepreneurship Theory and Practice* Vol. 17, 3

Senge, Peter (2006) *The Fifth Discipline: The Art and Practice of the Learning Organization.*

Stathis, Mike (2004) *The Startup Company Bible for Entrepreneurs.* AVA Publishing.

Suri, Rajan (1998) *Quick Response Manufacturing.* Productivity Press.

Index

14, *23*, 55, 61

innovation, 9, 11, 15–16, *23*, 29, 34–35, 38–39, 44
   See also change, capacity for

internal organizational planning, 1, 7–18, 22, 23, 25, 45, 47

intuition, 20

IT (information technology), 10, 11, *23*

key performance indicators, 17

knowledge management, 11–12, 14, *23*, 55, 61

lean manufacturing, 14, 39, 47

lean startup, 14

logic model analysis, 17, 23, 51

management
   disciplines of, 10, 13–14
   maturity model, 18–19
   tools and techniques, 16–17, 51–53, 62

management team
   consulting with employees, 23
   and corporate identity, 60
   corporate structure and, 8
   importance of experience, 3–4, 7
   keeping alignment with goals, 50
   management schema and, *23*
   and program execution, 56–59
   support for planning champion, 54

meetings, 2, 51, 54, 56, 61, 62

mergers, 45

mission statements, 16, 21, 23, *23*, 29, 30–*31*, *42*, 62

objectives, *23*, 48–*49*, 50, *52*–*53*

See also goals, strategic

operational plans
   defined, 1–2, 21–22, 24–25, 50–51
   failure of, 56–59
   internal, 9–12
   reviewing, 62
   See also strategic planning

operations, business, 9–10, *23*, 51

outsourcing, 9–10

performance management, 17, *24*

personnel. *See* employees

PESTLE scans, 35

planning, types of, 1–2, 21–25

planning champion, 54, 55–56, 59, *59*

principles of successful program implementation, 17, *23*, *24*, 60

product design, 11

program champion, 54, 59, *59*

program evaluation, 17, *24*

program execution, iv, 12, 13, 17, *24*, 56–69

project management, 17, *24*, 49–50

Quick Response Manufacturing™, 14

record-keeping, 11–12, *23*, 55, 61

relationships, special, 23, 27–28, 32–33, 37–38

research, planning, 23, 26–43, 54

research and development, 11, *23*

risk, 13, 23, *24*, 43, 47

round table session, 55–56

scalability, 3, 12

schema, generic planning and management, 2, 23–25

self-identification, 26–29

About the Author

Enterprise risk management consulting: risk assessment facilitation; ERM implementation; creator of online training.

Former Director of Human Resources and Strategic Planning; Specific Mechanical Systems, Victoria, BC. (Winner, Business of the Year 2015, Greater Victoria Chamber of Commerce).

Former Senior Manager, Enterprise Risk Management, Government of British Columbia. Facilitated solutions in multi-stakeholder projects.

Web presence:

Podcast, blog, books and online courses:
RiskCommentary.ca

Linked In profile:
https://www.linkedin.com/in/edward-robertson-801b5012

www.ingramcontent.com/pod-product-compliance
Lightning Source LLC
Chambersburg PA
CBHW022050190326
41520CB00008B/763